CW00550627

First published by Head Heart + Brain 2014
Second edition January 2016
157, 41 Millharbour, London E14 9ND. United Kingdom
www.headheartbrain.com

info@hhab.co.uk

British Library Cataloguing in Publication Data

A CIP catalogue record for this book is available from the British library

ISBN 978-0-9929007-5-5

1

About this book

This book provides the science related to a number of activities in business such as decision-making, change, team engagement and individual performance. We have added tips and tools to help leaders work in a way that is more consistent with what science teaches us. We have drawn on neuroscience, social psychology and behavioural economics. We believe by working in this way, leaders can lead their team and manage their own performance more successfully. Each section covers a number of topics. Pick a topic that addresses your issue, or take a different page each day, read the science and try out the tool or tip. You can also use the book to coach your team, use at team meetings to improve areas of performance or share with individuals who want to solve a particular performance issue. The tips and tools can be used with groups or individuals or applied to yourself.

Contents

BRAIN BASICS

Things every leader should know about the brain

Understanding other people

Our ability to collaborate, understand and engage with others is a special feature of humans. It allows us to work with others to create things that no single individual could. For this to happen, we have to be able to understand others. This is called the Theory of Mind or mentalizing.

We track the minds of others almost constantly and ascribe meaning to what we believe they are thinking. Biologically, there is an overlap between the regions activated when we are thinking about ourselves and thinking about others. This suggests that to create a hypothesis about others we first refer to our own thoughts and then project them on to the other person. Matthew Lieberman, a leader in social neuroscience at UCLA, found we switch to this circuit within seconds of stopping a cognitive task. It is the base-line activity of the brain, the default network.

What to do – The check-in process

Check-in is a useful way for business teams to begin meetings. It encourages participants to become fully present, for everyone to speak, and to hear what's on people's minds. It helps the leader understand where each team member is in the context of the meeting as each participant takes a turn to briefly share what is happening in "their world," what they are thinking and feeling, and what they want from the meeting. This allows each person to set aside preoccupations and to give their full attention to the group and the meeting.

Steps:

+ Give the group an appropriate question. The questions will, of course, vary based on the context
+ Ask people to pay attention to what is being said and to suspend their judgment
+ Role model open and honest sharing
+ Go around the group until everyone has been heard then begin the meeting agenda.

The threat response

From an evolutionary point of view it is fairly easy to see why our reaction to fear helped us to survive and thrive as a species; we could react quickly to danger. But, in modern day business, that same reaction can be a major hindrance. Research by the University of Wisconsin Madison found that whilst fear makes people more alert to the local environment it interferes with the ability to use the upper brain regions, the executive brain, and limits planning and decision-making.

When faced with a fearful situation participants had an enhanced functioning in circuits related to taking in visual information but a reduced capacity to make sense of that information. Removing the threat reversed the ability. The researchers believe our brain has developed to balance the different systems of automatic and rational reasoning. In threat situations the balance is disrupted.

What to do – Manage threats at work

Select something you are concerned about, like a high pressure situation or a change that you need to make.

Rate your confidence on a scale of 1-10 where one is deeply fearful and 10 is totally confident.

List the signals you get about the situation; including bodily feelings, self-talk and behaviour like procrastination to help you make the rating.

Step back mentally and breathe. Take three deep breaths and then refocus on the situation. Notice how you feel more in control.

Social pain

Research at UCLA by social neuroscientist Matt Lieberman and his wife Naomi Eisenberger came up with the rather surprising finding that the brain networks for physical pain are also used for social pain (the "pain" of rejection or humiliation, for example). Whilst social pain may feel different, just as the pain of a stubbed toe feels different to stomach cramps, the networks processing it in the brain are the same. Lieberman says the things that cause us to feel pain are things that are evolutionarily recognised as threats to our survival and the existence of social pain is a sign that evolution has treated social connection like a necessity, not a luxury.

The implication for leaders in business is that we should pay much more attention to the impact of social rejection: like giving feedback in public, challenging in social settings and disrupting bonded teams.

What to do – Manage social pain

Monitor just how careful you are about creating or acknowledging social pain. For example, how often do you:

+ Criticise in public?
+ Give negative feedback?
+ Challenge publically?
+ Exclude someone from a meeting or team event?

On the positive side, you can easily create social reward. Connection to a social group is critically important for emotional well-being; positive feedback about increased social reputation lights up reward pathways in the brain. Being treated fairly by others also increases activity in the ventral striatum and ventromedial prefrontal cortex, two key components of the brain's reward system.

Strategy and people

Organisations tend to focus on systems and processes, and this pushes leaders to think rationally rather than socially. Over time this rational thinking becomes a habit – it's the way things are done – and less and less attention is paid to social connections. Leaders will be missing lots of social cues, and the information and opportunities which could provide relational solutions to problems. They end up focusing on analytical solutions: "we just need to run the numbers." Yet many of the toughest business challenges require social solutions (engagement, motivation, productivity... to mention just three).

Interestingly, the degree to which your own medial prefrontal region has been active whilst reading this is indicative of how likely you are to discuss these ideas with other people.

What to do – Make more social connection

First of all understand your own habits: do you tend to focus more on strategy, logic and rational analysis or relational people matters? If you are not sure keep a log for a couple of weeks.

If you need to shift to more relational matters, work with someone who is naturally good at this and ask them to prompt or prime you to think about or notice the social impact before meetings, decisions and strategy planning.

Purpose and meaning

Dan Ariely, a behavioural economist from Duke University says that when we think about how people work, the naïve intuition we have is that people are like "rats in a maze." We have a simplistic view of why people work and what the labour market looks like; our intuition is that we exchange time and skills for money. But when you look carefully at the way people work, you find there's a lot more at play. Ariely provides evidence that we are also driven by meaningful work, by others' acknowledgement and by the amount of effort we've put in: the harder the task is - the prouder we are, the more recognition - the more meaningful the work feels.

What to do – Creating meaningful work

Identify what you/the team are passionate about for the company. Write this down. Based on these two to three passions define the benefits they will bring to the company and the outcomes that they will achieve. Write a short description which encapsulates your purpose at work based on these passions and outcomes. The best purpose statements have sticky characteristics:

+ They convey something in a way that is simple and straightforward
+ They use surprise, interest and curiosity to get attention
+ They connect with what we can see, hear, feel, smell and taste
+ They are believable - testable against your own/others experience
+ They create an emotional connection.

Emotional contagion

Your behaviour can energize or deflate your entire team through emotional contagion; if you are relaxed and positive and set an upbeat tone, you'll trigger similar feelings and behaviours among your team. Shared mood unites a team, and teams with positive joint experience perform better. Emotional contagion stems from neurobiology. Positive behaviours, such as empathy, create a chemical connection between a leader's brain and the brains of others. By managing those interconnections well, leaders can deliver better measurable business results. For example, Goleman and Boyatzis found that after one executive worked with a coach and role model to improve her behaviour, employee retention and emotional commitment soared in the team and the unit's annual sales jumped 6%.

What to do – Monitoring your emotions

One way to monitor your emotions and how they may be impacting the team is to keep an emotional diary or journal. Keeping track of how you are feeling each day and in different circumstances will enable you to track the good days and the not so good days. Knowing the triggers that generate the type of day you have will enable you to mitigate those that put you into a poor frame of mind. Difficult days are unavoidable but you can shift your mood by acknowledging the issue and moving on. Physically removing yourself from the source of the problem can also be helpful.

Emotions matter

Emotions drive our subsequent behavioural response. In an experiment, faces that were initially seen as angry were rated as more angry on a subsequent viewing. The researchers also found that participants imitated the emotion with their own faces when viewing the pictures again, showing how the emotion on the face was perceived automatically. This research suggests the initial interpretation will drive subsequent feelings about the person and behavioural reactions to them.

What to do – Check your inferences

The ladder of inference helps to check assumptions which will drive your expressions. We rarely test these assumptions and beliefs which then act as a filter for subsequent information. This blinds us to other possibilities and interpretations of new data or different interpretations of events.

As a leader, become more aware of your own thinking. For example:

+ Listen to your internal dialogue and check its relevance
+ Make your thinking and reasoning more visible to others, state your assumptions
+ Ask questions about the reactions you observe in others
+ Inquire into others' thinking and reasoning
+ Check out your "mind-reading" by asking questions. *"What was the reason for your suggestion?"*
+ Use open questions to encourage others to check their own assumptions.

Managing emotions

Leaders use different methods to manage emotional responses. One of the most studied is reappraisal or reframing. Experiments vary but all hinge around asking people to assess an emotional event, a video or picture. Their emotional arousal is then measured. They are then told a different 'story' about the scene and the emotional response is again measured. So for example, a picture of a group of people crying outside a church may be assumed to be a funeral. When it is reframed as a wedding, the emotional impact changes too. The scans found that when people reappraise, areas in the prefrontal cortex associated with cognitive control are active and areas like the amygdala become less active. The opposite occurred when people were asked to just become aware of their feelings. Reframing the meaning of the event can reduce the emotional impact.

What to do – Reframe events

Reframing is one way of dealing with negative interpretations of a difficult situation or change.

The trick is to ask yourself "is this the way it is or could it be different?"

+   How do you know this is the only interpretation?
+   What specific evidence do you have?
+   How have you made meaning of the data?
+   How might someone else see the data? What else could the data mean?
+   What assumptions are you making? What are you missing?
+   What else could be true?

False consensus

We find it hard to believe that others think differently to us. If we know or believe something we assume others do too, others must hold the same beliefs. This is the False Consensus Effect. Neuroscientist, Jason Mitchell, undertook a number of experiments that showed if we see ourselves as similar to others we believe others think like us. What is more, we tend to extend our assumptions to unrelated areas. For example, we assume someone who we perceive to be similar to us will also like the things we do, such as foods or sports. This is not rational. The same happens if we perceive the person is different to us, we generalise the differences.

Leaders must guard against a tendency to assume their team think the same as they do and rather tap into the diversity of beliefs and experience.

What to do – Avoiding the False Consensus Effect

Avoiding False Consensus and working to engage people based on their own beliefs is part of a leader's role. Checking your assumptions is a useful way of avoiding False Consensus. This is easier to do with the help of another person. Choose someone who is not afraid to challenge you and to express different views:

+ Make a note of your views on the problem or topic
+ Note your assumptions
+ Test the views and assumptions by sharing them with someone else
+ Note the differences. These may be subtle and it is important to probe below the surface assumptions.

This is a useful process to run at the beginning of projects and when problem solving.

Empathy

When you empathise you signal that you deeply understand the other person. This has been described, by neuroscientist Dan Siegel, as our human 'need to be felt.' As we are social beings, it makes sense that empathy is a need we all experience. When we are empathetic, different parts of the brain are activated in a number of steps:

Thinking about empathy activates the prefrontal cortex and you begin to plan and set intentions. This also alerts the limbic system.

There is an opening of the mind and usually a relaxation of the body. This activates the mentalizing or default networks which think about yourself and others. We understand others based on our understanding of ourselves.

What to do – Activating empathy

We often move to an empathetic state without consciously being aware of it yet at other times it is hard to achieve. When this is important use these steps:

+ Prepare yourself by imagining you are already in a state of empathy; remember what it feels like in your body and how you think about it
+ Quiet your internal dialogue. Concentrate on understanding the other person. This achieves both the goal of empathy and the goal of quieting your mind
+ If you notice your mind wandering bring your attention back to the other person
+ Focusing your gaze softly on the other person helps, as does focusing on the emotion behind the content of the conversation.

Honest signals

Psychology has for many years emphasised the importance of body language and tone of voice in successful communication. This is largely intuitive but research from Sandy Pentland at MIT is able to verify and even put numbers on these factors, using an electronic badge. He has found that we act on and are influenced by the "honest signals" people send. This is unconscious and includes 'reading' non-verbal language including tone and energy. Honest signals contrast with "dishonest" signals such as when people are pretending, to be interested, for example.

Pentland says the ability to communicate "honest signals" is a significant factor in the success of individuals and teams, and can account for as much as 50% of the success of a group. Pentland calls people who master their honest signal "charismatic connectors." They talk to everybody and drive the conversation around a team. They mainly work to connect people and information.

What to do – Creating honest signals

This is a useful tool to use with the team at a meeting or off site to help them understand the benefits of honest signals and to be better able to access their own.

Get people to shake hands with the other participants while imagining that the person they are shaking hands with is going to be difficult to deal with. Notice their reaction and body posture. Then have them walk around the room and pick someone to shake hands with whilst imagining that the person is a great friend who will help them in many ways. The difference is always profound and it demonstrates (among other things) that what you are thinking changes the signals you give off.

Power cues

Nick Morgan's book *"Power Cues"* describes the science behind how we show up to others. He describes seven cues. We believe the most important are:

> **Self-awareness** - how do you show up when you walk into a room? What do you convey with your body?

> **Other-awareness** – what unconscious messages are you receiving from others?

> **Your voice** - do you have a leadership voice?

> Your **beliefs and assumptions** - is your unconscious mind holding you back or propelling you forward?

What to do – Practice power cues

Self-awareness: See Confident behaviours (following)

Other-awareness: We are already experts, but at an unconscious level; how consciously aware are you of the messages that you are picking up from other's behaviour? To what extent do you recognise and understand what others are thinking before they themselves know it? Test your awareness by checking your assumptions with others or simply asking others what they are feeling.

Your voice: This is something that you might take for granted and rarely think about. But it is one of the primary ways in which you connect with and influence people every day. To what extent are you aware of how you use your voice? Record your voice or ask for feedback from a trusted person.

Beliefs and assumptions: Are you aware of the stories you tell yourself, "I always go blank under stress," "I tend to choke when the boss is pressuring me to speak up." To what extent do you replace these repeated ideas with winning ones?

Confident behaviours

How you stand matters! If you want to be successful, research by Amy Cuddy, found that adopting a more confident stance increased testosterone (the hormone linked to power and dominance in humans) and lowered cortisol, the stress hormone (linked to hypertension, memory loss and reduced cognitive functioning).

We often form habits related to how we stand, talk and project ourselves with certain people. Check your body language is giving the signal you desire to be influential. You can also give yourself a boost of confidence before an important meeting by adopting a power stance.

What to do – Power pose

Amy Cuddy found that adopting a power posture for around two minutes regularly can change self-perception and the perception of others.

When you need to be confident, and want others to think you are, spend a few minutes in a power pose. It sounds silly, but stand like superman; legs wide and hands on hips. Or sit back with your hands behind your head and your feet up on the desk. Or make a pose as though you are crossing the finishing line in a 100 meters race. Take up more space with your body by being expansive.

Your physiology will release those hormones and you will start to feel confident. Then go ahead with your presentation, meeting or whatever you need to do.

New ways of thinking

The brain has evolved for efficiency and routinely takes perceptual shortcuts to save energy. Perceiving information in the usual way requires little energy and so if possible we will think about something in the same familiar way. So for example, we think about coat hangers as a tool to hang clothes. Depending on how creative you want to be they could be used for picking locks, as a car aerial, or a piece of art.

Only by forcing our brains to re-categorize information and move beyond our habitual thinking patterns can we begin to imagine truly novel alternatives.

What to do – Changing thinking habits

The antidote is personal experience: seeing and experiencing something first-hand can shake people up in ways that abstract discussions around conference room tables can't.

It can be extremely valuable to start creativity-building exercises or idea generation efforts by taking a visit outside the office, by engineering personal experiences that directly confront our implicit or explicit assumptions.

Encourage your team to visit customers' premises; networking with leaders in other organisations; talking to customers about their experience of your product or service are just a few examples of how to facilitate a different way of thinking.

Stories and the brain

Intriguing research shows how stories impact rapport. A research study recorded a women's brain whilst she was telling a story and also recorded the brain activity of those who were listening to her. The images showed that the listeners' brain activity began to mirror the storyteller's brain patterns. Researchers also measured the listeners' comprehension of the story and found that the better the comprehension the closer the brain mirror. Even more intriguing, in those with the highest comprehension, their brain activity preceded the speakers, suggesting that those listeners anticipated the content of the story. The study suggests that this mirroring is not just the result of the rapport but the very basis on which we communicate. We have to couple our brains to understand each other.

What to do – Constructing stories

Before you use a story to get your point across consider the purpose. Stories come in different types. Some to consider are:

"Who I Am" stories - can give a powerful insight into what really motivates you

"Why I'm Here" stories - the goal, here, is to create trust

"Vision" stories - tell these to inspire hope, especially during change or difficult situations. A vision for where you are going and how it will be different can pull the team towards it

"Values in Action" stories - illustrate what you believe rather than preaching

"I Know What You're Thinking" stories - in business the advantage of telling this type of story is that you can anticipate another person's objections, and then show why those objections aren't applicable in this situation.

The envy tightrope

Whilst we are rewarded by social connections, science also reveals the tightrope leaders must walk between connecting with their team and generating feelings of envy. The science suggests that envy is a universally painful emotion. Envy includes feelings of inferiority when comparing with those who are perceived as similar but more advantaged in some relevant way. This leads to feelings of pleasure when others experience misfortune. This feeling has been termed Schadenfreude. Studies found that when something good happened to a person they saw as similar and more advantageous, the pain regions of the brain were activated. But when something bad happened to a similar person, it activated the reward regions.

What to do – Connection verses envy

Consider how well you do the following:

+ Use 'we'
+ Create opportunities for interaction and get to know people personally
+ Create a climate of trust
+ Focus on what the group has achieved, rather than problems
+ Involve people in planning and creation of the vision for the group
+ Keep people informed even when it is not necessary for their particular role
+ Take some risk with developing people
+ Verbally reward, praise people.

TEAM PERFORMANCE

Including trust, motivation, feedback, reward and engagement

Team bonds

You know the feeling - the team just doesn't gel! Science is telling us why. Our brains are wired to categorise things, including people. We do this instantly and unconsciously. Those people perceived as similar to us become our in-group. Those people perceived as different from us become our out-group. Once categorised, we filter information based on the group we have assigned others to and this can have long lasting implications for the team dynamic. Luckily, our definition of in-group and out-group changes with different circumstances, so check you are undertaking interventions that break any barriers down and create common goals across the teams you want to work together.

What to do – Bond teams together

For your team to work effectively, you need to minimise in-group and out-group feelings. Sometimes just the awareness that this happens is enough for people to modify their behaviours and realise they are treating some people differently. At other times, you need to overcome the unconscious categorisation:

+ Take time for introductions and induction of new people
+ Create a common goal across the groups
+ Make sure people get to know each other
+ Share personal information
+ Get individuals helping others to achieve the common goal
+ Remember to have social events from time to time
+ Look for similarities to build common ground.

The mind-set for success

Carol Dweck has studied the mind-set of success. She found people with a fixed mind-set assume their intelligence and talents are innate. They were born with them. People with a growth mind-set assume they can improve through working hard, practice and learning.

These two mind-sets impact on work performance, when there are setbacks or challenges that have no clear answer. A growth mind-set encourages exploration and persistence.

Leaders tend to hold beliefs about which mind-set exists in their employees. This has implications for culture and especially for performance management and development of staff. For example, do you hire for potential (growth mind-set) or for capability (fixed mind-set)?

What to do – Creating a growth mind-set

First of all notice your own preference. Mind-sets are a tendency rather than being fixed forever. Then think about the characteristics you need in your business. If this is for more of a growth mind-set, Carol Dweck's research has shown you can change through the language you use and actions you take:

+ Praise effort not accomplishment
+ Coach on tactics not just results
+ Encourage experimentation
+ Encourage people to take some risk in their career
+ Allow people to fail and understand the learning
+ Run post-project reviews and focus on learning.

The qualities of successful teams

Sandy Pentland at MIT has invented a wearable electronic sensor to measure exactly what good communication involves, in real time. His "sociometric badge" captures *how* people communicate, not *what* they say. In his study, the more successful people were more energetic; they talk more, but they also listen more; they spend more face-to-face time with people and pick up cues from them; they draw people out, and get them to be more involved with the team.

Pentland's data identifies what makes for effective communication and connection between people, such as in a team meeting, or presenting a proposal. Pentland's findings support the notion that these types of social factors like tone of voice, body language and energy are as important as intelligence or other factors in productivity.

What to do – Managing team dynamics

Pentland's three most important factors for team productivity and cohesion are:

> **Energy:** how team members contribute to the team as a whole
>
> **Engagement:** how team members communicate with each other
>
> **Exploration:** how team members communicate with others, especially those outside the team, bringing in new ideas.

Map the levels of each of these factors in your team. Pentland found there are usually a few people who are strong at all three factors. It is important that you have a cross- section of people carrying out the different factors and that there is time and resources which allow people to do so.

A high performance environment

Jessica Payne, at University of Notre Dame, has found the best environment for learning contains three inter-related elements:

A **degree of stress** to perform. Too little stress or arousal and people are complacent and lethargic. Too much stress and the functioning of the pre frontal cortex begins to close down, causing us to forget, panic and generally struggle to perform.

A **positive mood** aids learning, memory, insight and the executive functions in the pre frontal cortex. It also enables people to understand a broader perspective, make connections and solve problems more creatively.

The final element is **sufficient sleep**. Sleep is essential for maximising consolidation of memory. It also aids our ability to make connections and improves decision-making for insight-type problems.

The research also suggests that the elements of high performance are inter-related and an improvement in one area will improve others.

What to do – Creating a high performance environment

As a leader, be aware of the quality of the environment you are creating:

+ How can you create an environment which aligns sleep, mild stress and positive mood in your business?
+ What are the areas where you need to change the culture or set a better example?
+ How can you pass these messages on to others? This includes the way you tolerate or model out-of-work behaviours, like late night email or conference calls.

Building an engaged team

Not surprisingly, all the research indicates that the leader's approach makes a huge difference to the team's level of engagement! How can you use what we know about the brain to ensure your approach is motivating and not sapping? There is no one piece of research, rather a number of studies that point the way:

+   Social needs are primary and the quality of relationships is critical; both across the group and with the leader
+   People categorise others unconsciously as either in-group or out-group and this impacts openness
+   People are primed to notice threat rather than reward and the leader's style can trigger either
+   Different environmental factors influence levels of attention, memory and ability to work productively.

What to do – Creating engagement

Providing a relatively socially connected, stress free, equitable work environment creates engagement. Check your approach as a leader:

+   Do you have cliques within the team? Who are the in-group and who are the out-group? What would bond people across these divisions? Have you created shared goals? What else do you need to change to role model 'one team'?
+   How focused are you on the relationships between team members? How do you create co-operation, harmony, and shared pride in work?
+   How does your leadership style contribute to a sense of reward? How might you be creating a sense of threat?
+   What are the levels of trust? How can you enhance trust across the team?
+   How does the environment manage stress and create a positive mood?

Trust

Trust is a powerful tool in the leader's kit. It is the foundation of many factors including engagement, motivation, discretionary effort, and creativity. People will not take risks and suggest new ideas if they do not feel trust. Also trust takes time to build but can be undone quickly so think about how you build trust and keep it. Trust is built when the CORE elements are attended to and rewards created and threats mitigated. (See Achieving Change for more on CORE).

What to do – Creating trust

Go on a walkabout: Be open and engage in conversation.

Capture vital information: Learn about each employee's life.

Find similarities: Instead of focusing on differences, seek mutual interests.

Ask for ideas and feedback: Ask what people need to perform their jobs better. Acknowledge that you hear their opinions.

Acknowledge progress and milestones: In many organisations, problems are solved, barriers are surmounted, tasks are completed... but progress is not noted.

Purpose is an effective motivator

A study, by Wharton's Adam Grant, involved a call centre at a university fundraising organisation. Grant randomly assigned employees to one of three groups. One group read stories from other employees describing the personal benefits of the job; financial, skills development and knowledge (Personal Benefit condition). Another group read stories from the beneficiaries of the fundraising, describing how the scholarships they obtained had a positive impact on their lives (Task Significance condition). The final group did nothing (Control condition).

The Task Significance group secured **more than twice** the number of weekly pledges (from an average of 9 to an average of 23) and **more than twice** the amount of weekly donation money (from an average of $1,288 to an average of $3,130). There was no change in the other groups' performance.

What to do – Know and share your purpose

As a leader know your transcendent purpose and share this with your team. Work with your team to help them clarify their purpose.

One way to do this is have them reflect on the following questions:

+ What am I passionate about for the company?
+ Based on these two or three passions define the benefit that they bring to others, our customers, society?
+ In a nutshell, what is my purpose?
+ Look for opportunities to remind them of their purpose on a regular basis.

Finally, as a leader, make sure you role model your commitment to your purpose. After all, we all know who would win if transcendent purpose met quarterly earnings in an alley on a dark night.

Feedback and the brain

We deal with vast amounts of information coming from the environment by unconsciously filtering it to make meaning. The area of the brain responsible for this has been called the default or narrative network because we tend to tell ourselves a story about what we are experiencing based on our interpretation of the information that we have chosen to focus on. We deeply believe our narrative and this determines our behaviour.

It also explains how individuals can experience the same thing in different ways and have a different perspective of events.

This has an impact when we give others feedback as it is likely that our interpretation may mismatch the individual's interpretation.

What to do – Giving feedback

Remember an individual's version of events may be different to yours. Be open to this and ask questions to discover how they perceive their performance. We always recommend getting the other person to give themselves feedback first. This minimises the threat response in the brain:

+ What's your feedback to yourself?
+ How do you think it has gone?
+ What has gone well?
+ What could you have done differently?
+ What did you learn?
+ If someone else was doing this what would your advice be to them?

By asking questions, you will help them to think differently about their performance and shift their interpretation. Also be open to shifting your own perspective.

Feedback and reputation

Despite the fact that our intention when giving feedback is positive, there is often an unintended side effect.

This is because of an unconscious response in our brain. When we receive feedback from others we experience this as a threat response - our sense of reputation and standing is impacted. This response happens at an unconscious level before we have had time to consciously process what has been said to us.

As a result, it can be surprisingly easy to accidentally threaten someone's sense of reputation by implying that you are of a higher social standing and as such are in a position to comment on their performance. This means that it is also possible to trigger a threat response when giving positive feedback unless you are careful with how you structure your words.

What to do – Mitigating a threat to reputation

Giving feedback without focusing on reputation can fail to deliver the required outcome and is likely to damage a person's motivation and engagement. Encouraging a person to seek information (feedback) about their performance can work. The trick is helping the person gain information that can boost their reputation or enable them to improve their performance and through this their standing:

+ Make a habit of seeking feedback yourself - act as a role model
+ Ask people what feedback they would give themselves at the end of a project or when completing a piece of work
+ Ask people what they have learnt from the project and what they would do differently next time
+ Ask if there are any areas they would like feedback on.

Feedback that works

The Progress Principle describes a study on how organisations sustain effective performance and high employee satisfaction. The study asked knowledge workers to keep a diary, over several months and record an event that stood out each day. From analysis of the diaries it was apparent the workers experienced three types of positive feedback:

+ **Nourishing events** that were uplifting. For example, when a boss praised them or provided emotional support
+ **Catalytic events** that helped work tasks, such as resources or training being provided
+ **Progress events** involving getting feedback on how they were making progress in meaningful work.

Significantly, employees' "best" days featured progress events. Next most satisfying were catalytic events and the least rewarding were nourishing events.

What to do – Giving effective feedback

This means it's worth saying "Good job!" to people (nourishing events). It's even better to give people resources and training (catalytic events). But if you want to maximise the impact on motivation and engagement, comment on progress towards a goal that is important to someone. When bosses praise progress, they remind employees that they're advancing and signal that it's noticed - all of which is consistent with a growth mind-set.

So, the answer to the thorny issue of feedback seems to be:

+ Focus on positive feedback
+ Focus it on progress made towards goals people value
+ Encourage employees to assess their own performance, and especially how they can do even better at what they're doing.

How well are you doing on feedback?

Equity and reward

Have you considered how fair your rewards are; salary and bonus as well as informal rewards and promotions? A number of studies on people's reaction to unfair rewards show people reject unfair offers even if this means getting less money, or nothing overall.

The area of the brain which is activated is the insula and is associated with experiencing distress and disgust. The more activity seen in this area, the more likely the person is to reject the offer. Lieberman found that when people were offered unfair rewards it was seen as a social insult but when enough monetary value was added people regulated their reaction to achieve a long-term gain over short-term insult; the brain areas associated with emotional regulation became more activated. The implication is that rewards that are perceived as unfair may be accepted but at a cost to the individual's state of mind, motivation and engagement.

What to do – Creating fair rewards

First and foremost is your reward system equitable? Check both informal and formal rewards:

+ Are payments clearly linked to contribution and based on criteria that people understand and can check for themselves?
+ Are your rewards fair compared to the market? Do you check the data regularly? Is it transparent to all employees and can you articulate your pay position compared to the market?
+ Do you have a clear reward philosophy or policy?
+ Do your performance measures cover both hard task and soft skills and attitudes?
+ Does everyone have access to the data and is the data cheat proof and hard to manipulate?

Social reward drives satisfaction

Studies in neuroscience and behavioural economics are raising questions about whether monetary rewards will ever, or were ever, the best way to motivate people. Not only are we pulling the wrong lever; we are neglecting important methods of motivating and engaging staff that cost nothing financially.

Neuroscience research shows people are motivated more by social rewards than by monetary reward. People experience physical pleasure when they are socially rewarded, for example, when people co-operate, when they give to others, have a good reputation and receive recognition. But people feel physical pain when they are excluded socially, are treated unfairly and where negative social comparisons are made. This data is being largely ignored in companies' compensation systems.

What to do – Creating social rewards

Dan Pink, in his book *"Drive, The Surprising Truth about Motivation"*, suggests that people expect to be treated to fair reward, but beyond that, money will not motivate discretionary effort. The neuroscience would largely agree with that conclusion.

Once financial compensation is deemed to be fair people crave a sense of purpose, a sense of options around how they work and to know that they are learning and developing personally.

All of these motivators are related to elements of the CORE model (more details in the section on change). Check you are rewarding people across the elements: **C**ertainty, **O**ptions, **R**eputation and **E**quity.

Learn to teach

The mentalizing system is active, like a reflex, whenever we're not engaged in a task or analytical thinking. And the more this network is activated when you are reading, hearing about an idea, or learning new things, the more likely you are to pass on the new information to other people. Learning with a view to helping other people activates this network. And it makes us more effective at learning than when we use our analytical brain. But it seems we can't do both at the same time.

What to do – Learning and teaching

Set the team up to help and mentor each other. Prime people to learn new ways of working or key messages by telling them they are going to teach others. You stand to gain in two ways:

Firstly your messages will get passed on more effectively.

Secondly people will feel a sense of engagement and reward from helping each other.

Coaching Charter

The way to get your team engaged is by using a coaching approach that is brain-savvy. A brain-savvy coaching approach includes:

Questions that are solutions focused - these help build a picture of the future action we would like to take. Doing this creates new brain networks, so that the desired action becomes familiar to us.

Get the **balance between ability and challenge** right - this leads to a state called Flow. This is the state when we do our best work. Ensure the proposed action is challenging, but not too challenging, in relation to the individual's perception of their level of ability.

When the individual **generates their own ideas,** they have an "aha" moment. The brain likes solving things and as a result, when we do this, pleasant chemicals are released in the brain, such as dopamine. At the same time, those chemicals engender a feeling of energy and help us feel ready to take action.

What to do – Follow the coaching charter

The Coaching Charter:

+ Solutions-focused
+ Balances perceived ability and perceived level of challenge (flow)
+ Allows coachee to generate own ideas
+ Reinforces insights
+ Creates new habits

The Coaching Charter aims to include questions and on-going support that will create new habits. (Also see the change section.)

Creating a strong virtual team

As we have evolved our brain has developed to encourage us to bond with those we see as similar to us, a friend or part of our in-group. We have a sense of threat when we encounter those we see as different, a foe or part of our out-group. Much of the early work on these ideas was applied to stereotyping and discrimination but there is now evidence that we do this all of the time at an unconscious level. Once we have categorised someone as foe or out-group it is hard to find a connection and we feel less empathy for those people.

Divisions within organisations sap energy and reduce productivity. This can be especially unhelpful when people need to work across cultures and in different physical locations. In these situations the leader needs to take extra care to create a strong in-group within the team.

What to do – Creating strong relationships

The best relationships at work go beyond a professional understanding. Real trust is developed when people know each other personally. This personal exchange is often lost when teams work remotely or the pace is busy, but is one of the keys to building trusting relationships that enable people to work productively. Do the following yourself and encourage it in the team:

+ Reveal something personal
+ Share some struggles and challenges
+ Talk about common non-work interests
+ Talk about shared values and goals
+ Get people talking about what is important
+ Use humour
+ Look for opportunities for the team to meet face to face.

The honest truth about dishonesty

Dan Ariely has found human beings want to be able to do two things at the same time. On the one hand, to feel good about themselves, but on the other hand to benefit from being dishonest. You might think that we can't do both, i.e. cheat and still feel good about ourselves. However, our ability to rationalise means we can. As long as we only cheat a little bit and have a story to rationalise our behaviour, most of us will cheat, but just a bit.

Dan Ariely, behavioural economist at Duke University, has undertaken many experiments and of 30,000 participants he found 18,000 little cheaters and only 12 big cheaters. We tend to focus on the big cheaters, but the cost to the organisation is greater when we combine the cost of all the little cheaters. Examples of little cheating might be going home early, claiming extra overtime, inflating sales, or taking home stationery...

What to do – Minimise dishonesty

Interestingly, Ariely found that when participants were reminded of some type of moral code they were much less likely to cheat, for example, when participants were asked to read the company ethics statement. He also found that when we are given the opportunity to open a new page and put past cheating behind us, we are more likely to behave honestly. As a leader, look for opportunities to:

+ Remind your team of company values and ethics
+ Have reminders of social and corporate responsibility
+ Look at your own behaviour and ask what story am I telling myself that allows me to cheat (just a little bit) and still feel good about myself
+ When a task has gone badly, give people the opportunity to start again and wipe the slate clean.

The best advice is give none

When things are changing people look for help but neuroscience has found giving advice can be risky. Dean Mobbs found that if our advice is rejected we can feel ostracised and disrespected. If it transpires that our advice was correct and the person rejecting that advice fails as a result, we can feel a fleeting sense of delight. Advice creates a host of defensive mechanisms including diminished guilt, hostility, and the use of explicit self-serving utterances such as "I told you so."

If our advice is accepted but then it ultimately turns out to be wrong, we can experience feelings of guilt. This guilt may arise from the fear of social exclusion, where these mistakes can lead to the group ostracising.

What to do – Insight over advice

Rather than give advice help the person come to their own insights and plan. The best way to do this is to ask powerful questions. These are questions that shift the other person's perspective and help them think differently about the change. Powerful questions tend to be open, short, start with what, when, how and are solution-focused rather than problem-focused.

Purpose and values

Most research on values - understanding what people value - starts with the neurochemical dopamine. This chemical determines how the brain processes reward and hence what is valued. Dopamine is found all over the brain. Two brain regions are important and used by neuroscientists to study value. One is the nucleus accumbens and the other is the ventral medial prefrontal cortex. They form a coherent system of value within the brain. The system is an old and all-purpose one that probably developed to provide motivation to find food, and shelter and other survival needs. The system has been adapted to other things that people find rewarding such as an attractive face, chocolate and money. This dopamine system is useful when we have to make decisions about where to put energy or what goals to pursue, especially when off-setting the value of one choice over another, like connecting to the team verses pursuing goals which benefit only ourselves.

What to do – Understand values conflicts

The reward system may be attuned to different things in a different context. What is of value now may not be of value in another context. Zaki has a three dimensional model of what is of value in different contexts:

Risk and safety - We are generally risk averse and so will make the choice of a reward now rather than risk more in the future.

Social connection verses social disconnection - Being liked by others is rewarding in and of itself.

Social comparison - We draw value from being good but also from being better than others.

These dimensions interrelate. Understanding what people value has a direct relationship to their performance.

ACHIEVING CHANGE

Responses to change, reducing resistance, gaining buy-in

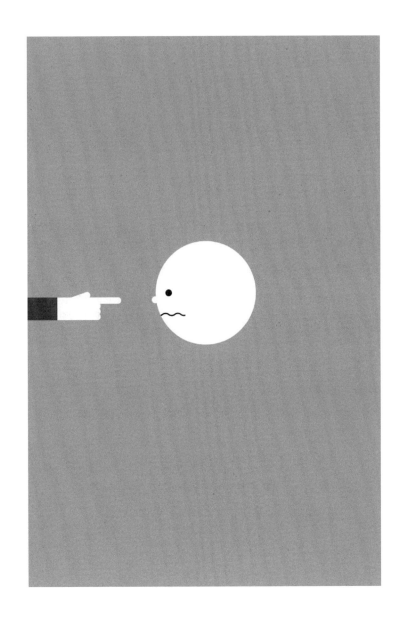

Changing behaviours

To achieve large scale change in business the majority of people need to change. To do this people must change work habits. Neuroscience shows that we have two broad ways of reacting to the world and to change. Via the *reflextive system*, which is automatic and based on habit and via the *reflective system* which is thoughtful or mindful. Neuroscientist Kevin Ochsner estimates that humans act on habit, the *reflextive system*, 70-90% of the time and are guided by deliberate mindful actions only 10-30% of the time. To change, people must create new habit. People need to set goals, create a strategy and maintain personal motivation to change behaviour. Helping people to think about the positive consequences of the change in the future helps to reduce cravings to act in the old way and helps them stay on track with goals.

What to do – Help to change habits

You can learn more about how habits are changed in later tips. It is worth knowing that it is easier to create a new behaviour than to change an old one.

Work out what behaviour will help you achieve the change and then create clear goals to achieve it. You are more likely to be successful when you:

> **Make your goal public**. We like to be seen to keep our commitments
>
> **Work with someone** else on the change
>
> **Plan for what might derail you**. See if/then goals
>
> **Reward yourself** for steps towards success.

Clear purpose

It sounds simple to be sure of your purpose or the team's purpose, but in highly charged change situations this can be hard to define, yet it is at this time that a clear purpose is most needed. It gives a sense of certainty and helps people understand their options and make choices.

Creating a clear purpose also helps focus goals, make decisions and guides behaviour. It gives people a sense of meaning which in turn helps engagement and motivation.

What to do – Creating a personal purpose

Steps:

+ Have each person draw a pictorial description of their future when the change is complete. Share the drawings
+ Have each person create a skyhook. The higher purpose of what they want to achieve
+ Identify what will be different once they have realised this. Make adjustments to their picture
+ Identify what it will take to make these changes. Have small groups help the individual complete their plan through supporting their ideas and challenging them if they become stuck

You may want to use this tool to create a group future purpose and plan by combining the individual images, skyhooks and plans.

Change tolerance

Whilst biologically the brain reacts to change in the same way, there are differences in how change-tolerant people are. One theory says this is related to the degree of arousal the individual experiences in the brain. The level of arousal is determined by the amount of catecholamine. The current understanding is that people need a degree of arousal to be motivated to act. Too little and people are lethargic, lacking motivation to achieve goals. Too much and people become over stressed resulting in a lack of focus, forgetfulness and feelings of panic. From a change perspective it could be that the base level of arousal of those tolerant of change is lower than those who find change difficult.

What to do – Increasing tolerance to change

Rather than see those who react strongly to change as difficult or performing poorly, understand what might be happening to them and consider how you can reduce the level of arousal. One way is to use the CORE model. Consider how each of the four elements of human social experience may be being threatened by the change and how you can mitigate or create a reward reaction in each element.

> **Certainty:** our confidence that we know what the future holds

> **Options:** the extent to which we feel we have choices

> **Reputation:** our relative importance to others (our social ranking)

> **Equity:** our sense of fairness

Certainty matters

In change there is often a reduction of certainty and the ability to predict what will happen.

The brain has been described as a pattern recognition machine. It looks for patterns. If the anticipated pattern is as expected, we feel a sense of reward and dopamine is released. If the pattern is not as expected, an error message is generated and discomfort is felt. This is the activation of the threat response; the feeling we get when something we were certain about does not happen or when situations feel ambiguous and we are in a state of flux.

The level of certainty impacts the way we make decisions. We take less risk when there is ambiguity about a situation. This has become known as the Ellsberg paradox. Uncertainty decreases reward and increases the emotional activity in the limbic system. This results in a built-in bias for certainty to avoid the sense of threat.

What to do – Creating more certainty

One of the characteristics of successful people is that they focus on what is in their control. What they CAN do. Next time you or the team are in an ambiguous situation and feeling out of control:

+ List all the things that may influence the successful outcome
+ Put a 'C' against the things you can control. The things you are certain about. Write down what you will do to ensure they contribute to your success
+ Place an 'NC' against those you can't control. Brainstorm what you CAN do to increase your control over them
+ Develop an action plan from the two lists to put you more in control
+ Put the NC thoughts to one side.

Using this process increases certainty and tolerance to change.

Options matter

Change often impacts the choice or control people have, for example over how they manage the impact of the change on their job.

Amy Arnsten studies the effects of limbic system arousal on prefrontal cortex functioning; when people feel they have no control and no options the prefrontal cortex functioning is reduced and in some cases shuts down completely. This is the feeling of a "blank mind." If people have choice or even the illusion of choice, cognitive functions are preserved. Even a small number of options or options which are not particularly attractive, can change people's perception of an event from stressful to tolerable. For example, options over office space can improve productivity. Helping people to retain options in a change situation is critical to reducing resistance and maintaining engagement and productivity.

What to do – Creating options

Dealing with a perceived lack of options is about changing your perspective on the situation. Some practical ways of changing your perspective of the options available in a situation are:

+ Change seats
+ Imagine you are very large - or small
+ Stand above the situation
+ Put yourself in someone else's shoes
+ Imagine you are seeing the situation as a film
+ Lie on your back (it's a good position to look up)
+ Imagine it is three months in the future and you are looking back on the current situation.

Reputation matters

A person's reputation is something of a mixed blessing in business. It is now clear, given that the workplace is a social environment, that relationships and hence social standing matters.

Studies have shown that people would prefer an increase in perceived reputation over monetary rewards. When reputation is increased people receive a boost of dopamine in the same way that they would for other rewards like praise, recognition, developing new skills and helping others. Being left out of a group can trigger a reduction in their perceived reputation and activate the same regions of the brain as experiencing physical pain.

How we perceive our relative reputation compared to others has consequences for how we react to others, are motivated and perform.

What to do – Increasing reputation

In change situations, reputation can be disrupted. Increasing perceived reputation can have positive benefits. Ask these questions of yourself and members of the team:

+ What are my sources of reputation?
+ What reputational sources am I most comfortable with?
+ What reputational sources am I least comfortable with?
+ What sources of reputation do I admire most in others?
+ What sources of reputation do I want to develop? How can I do this?

Equity matters

Change can generate a sense of inequity or unfairness, especially when it impacts people differently. Eisenberger found that all types of unfair treatment activated the same neurological pathways as being hurt physically. Other research found more sensitivity to a lack of equal treatment when the amount of serotonin, which is involved in feeling content, was manipulated. When participants had low commitment and low serotonin, they responded more strongly to unfair situations. This suggests that when people are tired, overworked or generally stressed they will be more alert to equity or will react more strongly, or both. Acts of fairness can create reward responses and an increased sense of trust.

What to do – Increasing fairness

To treat people equitably you need to understand their perspective. This technique is used in kindergarten in Japan to help children learn to take perspectives. It is call the "pillow" technique as people are positioned around a square, one on each side. The person on side:

+ A gives their perspective on an issue
+ B gives the perspective of the person you are seeking to understand better, like a customer
+ C listens carefully to both A and B and gives a complementary comment that combines into a new perspective
+ D listens to the three previous speakers, then offers something totally different - a thought, point of view, a new perspective that will shed a different light on the subject

Solution-focused

In complex change it is easy to get bogged down in problems. Our brain feels naturally more comfortable thinking about an existing problem. After all it is familiar and is something it knows well. Seeking solutions requires a step into the unknown especially if it is a novel solution. Yet in change situations, something new is what is most likely to move you forward. We can overcome the brain's natural reluctance and even give a shot of dopamine reward through focusing in on questions that move us towards solutions rather than further describing the problem.

What to do – Solution-focused questions

Think of a current problem that you are dealing with and make a brief note to remind you of the issue. Ask these questions of yourself:

+ What do you want?
+ How will you know you have got it?
+ What else in your life will improve when you have it?
+ What resources do you already have which can help you achieve this outcome?
+ What is something similar that you have succeeded in doing?
+ What is your next step?

These questions can also be used when coaching or in team problem-solving.

Make new ways of working stick

As people become more adept at a skill, the brain no longer needs to work as hard at it. The brain shifts to more automatic processing. Mastering a new skill results in decreased activity in brain regions involved in effortful control and attention and increased activity in the default network that is involved in self-reflective activities, including future planning or day dreaming. Thus, skill mastery is associated with increased activity in areas not engaged in skill performance, and this shift can be detected in the large-scale networks of the brain. Giving people time and rewards for working at new skills helps embed the changes required.

What to do – Developing mastery

To become really skilled it is important to keep the new skills or knowledge at the forefront of people's attention. People learn best when:

+ They have a clear idea of how the new skills or mind-set will help them be successful
+ The new skill is applied and practiced in multiple situations
+ They can apply the skill to current work
+ They have a plan to create new habits using the skills. Do this through, clear personal goals, repeated practice, and praise for success.

Change stories

It is possible that the reason stories are so powerful is that we think in narrative all the time. The area, known as the default system, called this because we default to using this area within a few seconds of not doing a task, processes how we think about ourselves and others. The area expresses thoughts as a narrative, a story we are telling ourselves. We think in narratives all the time. "I'll need to speak to John about the new project guidelines, and then tell Nancy we have a date for the management team off site…" There is a consistency in how we 'talk' to ourselves and how we tell stories. We make up stories in our heads for every planned action and conversation.

What to do – Successful stories

A story enables people to mentally rehearse the values and ideas being suggested. Telling a story is also a way of creating a deep connection with others. The characteristics of a story that will positively impact are based on the acronym "SUCCES" (with the last s omitted). Each letter refers to a characteristic that can help make an idea "sticky" that is memorable:

> Simple - find the core of any idea
> Unexpected - grab people's attention by surprising them
> Concrete - the idea can be grasped and remembered later
> Credible - make it believable
> Emotional - help people feel the importance of the idea
> Stories - empower people to use an idea through narrative.

Use this as a guide to create a more engaging and compelling way of getting your message across.

The Leader's Change Charter

We often hear leaders talk about resistance to change. This is a common term in change management. However, the neuroscience seems to suggest that it is not resistance but the brain which needs to be managed.

Helping people feel less threatened, setting clear goals and maintaining motivation are all helpful. Ways to do this are through what we call the Leader's Change Charter.

The charter encourages leaders to help people recognise the benefits of the change for themselves, creating insight into the benefits for them personally, reinforcing their ideas and helping people stay on track.

What to do – The Leader's Change Charter

Involve people in the design of the strategy and ways of working

Encourage people to generate their own ways of working within the broad strategy

Encourage personal insight through the use of good questions

Help people be solution rather than problem focused

Provide training and workshops which allow people to build on their existing skills and to develop new skills

Encourage people to create symbols or triggers which will remind them to undertake the new behaviour

Create multiple ways of reinforcing the new behaviours.

The language of change

Change is frequently described in emotional terms: the burning platform, do or die, sink or swim, the end of an era. The language we use may be descriptive but it also sends subliminal messages to the brain impacting levels of threat, motivation and creativity.

When describing change watch your language. Review formal communications for words that generate fear. Also remember some people are motivated by moving towards a vision of the future, others away from current problems.

What to do – Construct your language to motivate

Ensure your language and communications appeal to both preferences. So for example:

> "This change will create more flexibility for shift workers and give employees more control over work schedules." (Towards language).

> "This change will solve our problems with more efficient work schedules and shifts." (Away from language)

Galvanise support for the change

In any change there are people who respond in different ways. Recent research which models the impact of different types of organisations attempting change found that if 10% of people are fully on board with the change and deeply believe in it, they will convince others until there is a tipping point where people come on board. Below 10% and nothing will change. The research used models of different types of social networks:

+ A small company or business unit; each person connected to every other person.
+ A large company; everyone had roughly the same number of connections
+ Opinion leaders; a small number of individuals with a large number of connections

Initially each model had a mass of people holding a traditional belief but they were open to listening. The minority opinion holders were unshakable in their belief. It was the 'true believers' who convinced others to change, no matter what the network configuration.

What to do – Changing beliefs

Make sure you understand and have in place the right change agents. Consider who your change agents are and how they feel about the change. It is not necessary for them to be very senior. The quality of their belief is what matters.

Make sure you understand the number of people who agree with the change and truly believe in it. Make this one of the key measures. You need to achieve at least 10% of people who are true believers

Change network

Research found that having a change agent with the right shaped network was crucial to successful change. For divergent change that challenges deeply help values and beliefs in the organisation, you need agents who have a bridging network which is spread out but means they can influence across different departments and functions.

Incremental change that builds on values and norms of the company needs a change agent with a cohesive network. People in this network are closely connected to one another. This builds trust and mutual support.

What to do – Using change networks

Make sure you have in place the change agents with the right type of network for the change you must make. It is not necessary for them to be very senior.

The **bridging network** provides diverse knowledge and relationships across the organisation and puts the agent in a position to make sense of the change to the different business units. They also have the trust of scattered people giving better control over what, when and how the change is introduced.

The **cohesive network** means people are closely connected, trusted and support each other. People want to stick together and help each other. This introduces social pressure to move together to achieve the change, or block it if the agent is not on board.

DECISION-MAKING AND PROBLEM-SOLVING

Including decision bias and brainstorming

Positivity

Extensive work over many years by Barbara Fredrickson has found the many beneficial effects of positive emotions. In the context of problem-solving and decision-making, a positive mood and team environment have been shown to create more insight, produce more creativity and a team that performs to a higher standard as measured by goal achievement and strategy execution.

Fredrickson says that it is important to achieve a ratio of 3:1 positive experiences to negative experiences. This ratio seems to be the optimum. People and teams then are more open to new ideas as the brain goes into approach or reward mode and this results in people picking up more contextual information, making more connections and being better able to read the emotions of others.

What to do – Understand your positivity ratio

Fredrickson has found that positivity builds up over time and also helps to create resilience. This is an opportunity to measure and monitor your own levels of positivity. You can do Fredrickson's Positivity Test on her website www.positivityration.com. She also suggests analysing over time to get a sense of your ratio, this helps to avoid distortion by remembering only the bad stuff, or the good stuff if that is your preference.

Knowing where you and the team are is the first step to change.

Emotional versus rational

Although we think our rational brain is in charge, our emotional brain is more involved in decision-making than we realise. Research by Antonio Damásio has found that it's not just logic that is needed for making decisions, emotion is at the heart of every decision we make. We talk about decisions that feel right and it is impossible to make decisions without some degree of emotion. Making decisions is not a matter of heeding one 'brain,' the rational or emotional brain, and ignoring the other. The brain has developed to work as a whole, integrating both its analytical and emotional capacities.

What to do – Take the middle path

The best approach to take when making decisions is a middle path in which we use both head and heart. Over time, observe the patterns of *how* you think under different circumstances. It means bringing more of your thought process into your conscious awareness:

+ Notice the content of your thoughts. What kind of language do you use to talk to yourself - is it kind, harsh?
+ Does the language vary, if so when?
+ What's your decision-making style - do you tend to over-analyse, generalise or cut to the chase of a problem?
+ How does the style change in different circumstances or for different types of decision?

Decisions and stress

Fear and excessive stress are both big obstacles to making smart decisions. When you are stressed, it affects your ability to hear what is being said and your body starts to release cortisol which reduces the effectiveness of the prefrontal cortex (our higher brain which is involved in decision-making). This interferes with our ability to learn, remember, and use the rational elements of decision-making. That's why in some stressful situations, you may go completely blank, jump to conclusions, or become impulsive.

What to do – Manage stressful decisions

One way to manage stress and its impact on decision making is to reappraise your experience. Use these ideas:

+ Consider tough decisions when you are mentally rested
+ When you are anxious about your mental performance, tell yourself "that's just my brain" this will enable you to step back and be more objective
+ Make changes to your thinking patterns - consider using mindfulness, whether it's meditation or just simply noticing what you are feeling.

(See Managing emotions - recognising what you are experiencing and labelling the cause of your anxiety will help reduce it)

Decision bias

Biases have a way of creeping into decision-making. As a leader you evaluate people, products and services on a regular basis, but how confident are you that you're fair and unbiased in your judgements and decisions? Many biases are completely unconscious to the individual, they are intuitive.

Research by Daniel Kahneman shows that we have two thought systems; one is a fast instinctive and emotional brain system and the other a slower, more deliberate and logical brain system. Often when we make decisions, our fast intuitive system jumps to conclusions or takes shortcuts that the more rational system doesn't question.

What to do – Test for bias

You can help to avoid bias by building in checks and balances:

+ Test your decision for bias by asking others perspective
+ Take time to reflect and review additional date
+ Sleep on important decisions
+ Test your intuition

In short find ways to engage your slower, logical brain.

The relative importance

Dan Ariely has completed a number of experiments that suggest we never make a decision based on its merits alone but on its relative merits compared to other options. It is always a relative choice. He has also shown that our mind-set and the options presented impact the decision. For example if you have the choice of three types of subscription to a magazine: one on line - the cheapest option, one print and one offering print and online access for the same price as the print version. In this scenario most people go for the print and online package but when the print only option is not shown most people pick the online only option. The additional option influences decision-making even when it is not objectively attractive.

What to do – Test your decisions

Consider how this preference may influence your own choices and decisions. The way to combat this is first to be aware of the preference. Secondly ask someone to test your thinking about your choice and how much you will actually benefit from what you have decided; how much will you use the subscription for example?

Decision defaults

Decision bias has brought our attention to the irrational ways in which we make decisions. For example countries which have similar cultures, have very different statistics on people who give organ donations. Dan Ariely says this is nothing to do with culture. Countries with high levels of organ donation have a different means of enrolling people to be donors. Those countries with a form that says tick the box if you want to donate; they get very few donators. Countries that ask people to opt out have much higher rates. The environment where we make decisions impacts our decisions much more than our rational thinking. The path of least resistance is the path most usually taken. When decisions are complex we tend to do nothing and take the easy option. We believe we make decisions but often we stick with what is our current activity or the easy option.

What to do – Make complex decisions easy

We tend not to believe that this is how we make complex decisions because we make a story, a rationale for why we have decided in a particular way. In your own team look at how people behave rather than their explanation. On the other hand knowing this can help you to position your ideas in a way that helps people take the path of least resistance when it fits your needs. For example have people opt out rather than opt in to the decision.

Loss aversion

Amos Tversky and Daniel Kahneman coined the phrase "loss aversion" in a series of studies. The term refers to our tendency to strongly prefer avoiding losses to acquiring gains.

This explains why when we have invested in something, be it emotionally, financially or our time, we find it difficult to make decisions that would result in any loss. A good example might be tolerating poor performance; the loss of our investment in that person makes us less likely to make a decision about dealing with the poor performance.

What to do – Checking your investment

When you are struggling to make a decision consider the following:

+   What are you losing?
+   How much time, money, and emotion have you invested?
+   Might your decision be biased due to what you will lose?

Work with someone else to help you be more objective about this decision.

Decision fatigue

We reach a certain point of the day when the quality of our decisions reduces. We begin to make poorer decisions and choices due to the brain's resources being depleted. Experiments by psychologist Roy Baumeister have demonstrated that there is a finite store of mental energy for exerting self-control and making quality decisions. With each decision we make throughout the day, the harder it is for our brain to continue to make decisions which are of a good quality. In other research, Eliot Berkman has found that motivation may be the key rather than depletion of resources.

What to do – Managing fatigue or motivation

To ensure you make the best decisions follow these guidelines:

+ Avoid back-to-back meetings that require focus and decision-making. Take short breaks and refreshments
+ Make the most important decisions earlier in the day or after a break when your mind is more alert and you have more energy
+ Avoid trying to focus on too many things at once. Focus your attention on one thing at a time - use lists; once it's written down, you've created some head/thinking space
+ Don't be afraid to "sleep on it." The height of decision fatigue can lead to making the easiest possible decision – no decision at all.

Think about your thinking

Research at University College London throws light on this skill which is one of the key ingredients of self-awareness. They found that people who were better at this showed increased grey matter volume, implying more neuron cell bodies. They also found enhanced integrity and efficiency of the neuronal fibres that connected the anterior prefrontal cortex to other brain regions. The research suggests but cannot confirm that it may be possible to train people to improve their meta-cognition, their thinking about thinking. Studies of mindfulness have already shown change is possible through practice.

What to do – The STOP tool

It is easier to review thinking, decisions and judgments when you can step back. As mentioned, this is one of the skills developed by mindfulness.

Another more instantaneous tool is STOP, created by Timothy Galway:

Step back

Think

Organise thoughts

Proceed

Know what type of problem you need to solve

Some surprising findings are emerging about problem- solving and creativity which contradict current practice in business. Scientists divide problems into two broad types: those that have a logical answer and those which do not. There are different ways of solving each of these types of problems. For example, thinking aloud about a problem works for analytical problem-solving but not where you need to gain insight. Doing this produces a mental set which hampers creative solutions. Similar mental sets occur when, for example, we try to solve problems with others. In other research Prof Jai and Karpen found that putting distance between the problem solver and the issue, such as imagining the issue occurred in another university, helped to create more creative solutions.

What to do – Create psychological distance

It is possible to induce a state of psychological distance by getting people to change the way they think about a problem. Techniques such as:

+ Imagining the problem is happening far away
+ Putting yourself in others' shoes
+ Thinking of the problem as unlikely
+ Imagining the problem is in the past.

For additional ideas see Brainstorming and Insight.

Dealing with complexity

Holding a complex concept in your brain involves activating the visual circuitry. Robert Desimoney discovered that the brain is capable of holding only one representation of a visual object at a time. Remember the optical illusion, whereby a vase or a face can be seen, but not both at once.

When we are thinking about something complex, we try to hold dozens of variables in our mind. What happens in practice is we quickly switch between one variable and another. This is tiring and reduces our ability to make connections.

What to do – Managing complexity

Follow these guidelines, when dealing with something complex:

+ Simplify information by approximating and focusing on an idea's salient elements
+ Group information into chunks whenever you have too much information. Name the chunk to represent the content
+ Practice getting your most important ideas in mind first, not just the ones that are easiest
+ Create a visual representation of the idea such as a mind map or collage

Brainstorming

The typical way of flushing out the solution to a problem has been in a group brainstorm.

Research by Schooler has shown that people produce a 'mental set'- a narrow way of thinking about the issue or problem when they are asked to think aloud or discuss solutions in a group. He suggests that creative thinking is constrained by exposure to other people's ideas. Groups can get directed towards a particular solution or develop an assumption about the scope or approach to solving the problem.

What to do – Solving complex problems

If you need to solve a complex problem or be creative, first define a question as a group, then ask individuals to take time out and do something interesting but simple for a while. This allows the non-conscious brain to do the solving/creativity piece for you.

Then ask individuals to write down their ideas before coming back as a group to share their ideas.

Groups using this approach were found to be able to generate more ideas, to generate better ideas, and to better discern the quality of the ideas they generated.

The Ikea Effect

Dan Ariely talks about the "Ikea Effect" which refers to the impact that creating something personally has on our perception of its value. If you have ever bought furniture from Ikea and gone through the arduous process of putting it together you will probably identify with the idea that once created you look upon it with love.

He explored this by conducting a series of experiments using Origami and Lego. Those who had invested effort in creating something rated their outputs more highly than those who were asked just to rate the objects.

There are pros and cons with the "Ikea Effect." The upside is that when the team is creating something, they buy-in to it. The downside is that they lose objectivity and think it is better than it might be and are reluctant to let it go when change occurs.

What to do – Using the pros and avoiding the cons

The "Ikea Effect" applies to change, creating new ideas and introducing new policies and processes. To take advantage of the pros, get your team engaged and on board with an idea by involving them in its creation.

To avoid the cons, remember that when your team, and by the way that means you, are invested in something the assessment of its value can be exaggerated.

Use analogies to stir imagination

In testing and observing 3,000 executives over a six-year period, Professors Clayton Christensen, Jeffrey Dyer, and Hal Gregersen, noted five important "discovery" skills for innovators. These were associating, questioning, observing, experimenting, and networking. The most powerful overall driver of innovation was associating - making connections across "seemingly unrelated questions, problems, or ideas."

What to do – Stirring the imagination

Use the following analogies to spark ideas around innovating your data, customer interactions, cost efficiencies, supply chain or loyalty programme:

+   How would Google manage our data?
+   How might First Direct engage with our consumers?
+   How could Easy Jet cut our costs?
+   How would Zara redesign our supply chain?
+   How would Tesco design our customer loyalty programme?

Creating insight

Studies by Mark Beeman and others have provided clues as to how we might increase an 'aha' moment to solve a complex problem or make a decision. These 'aha' moments are when the solution comes to you suddenly and is surprising, but you are also sure it is right. You get better insights when you're able to notice 'weak activations' or 'quiet signals' in the brain.

We only notice signals that register above the base line of noise in the brain. So, just as it's hard to hear a quiet cell phone at a loud party, it's hard to notice signals that have less energy than the general energy level already present in the brain. Quietening the overall activation of the brain requires minimising anxiety (which is why we have better ideas when we feel happy) and reducing general brain activity.

What to do – Allowing ideas to emerge

In order for an insight to occur, think about your thinking:

+ Broadly research the issue or project well in advance
+ Reduce your anxiety any way you can
+ Try letting your mind become idle. You're aiming for the easy, unfocused mental state like that which occurs as you drift awake in the morning when ideas dreamily flow into mind
+ Go for a walk, grab a coffee, do something totally different for a few minutes - see if an answer springs to mind

When you do have your insight make sure you capture it. Insights can be fleeting.

Brain bottlenecks

The brain seems to process information and ideas in a serial manner; one after another. When you procrastinate on a decision you can create a bottleneck. Something that is unresolved, which you keep coming back too or which interrupts your thinking and decision-making on a new matter. These half thought through issues eat up brain resources as you swing backwards and forwards, go off at tangents and then need to return to the decision stuck in the decision path. Almost like a conveyer belt, when one idea gets stuck it impacts the whole production line.

What to do – Avoid bottlenecks

+ Break down complex ideas into smaller chunks, the brain seems to do this automatically so you can take advantage of this by chunking information for easier storage and retrieval. The small chunks should be easy to understand and remember the information relevant to the decision.

+ Simplify information, particularly conceptual information into simple points which are easier to retain and quick to understand. This is why initials like PFC can be helpful, once you have internalised the bigger concept of the pre frontal cortex.

+ Prioritise what you need to do now and what can be left to later. To do lists help with this as they get things out of your PFC and save you trying to hold ideas in short-term memory. Getting them on to paper or your device means you can revisit them when you are ready.

So the old saying "deal with something once to be productive and efficient" is true. It always surprises me how old wisdom understood the brain in ways we sometimes seem to have forgotten.

THE SCIENCE OF CREATING AND ACHIEVING GOALS

Including setting, maintaining and rewarding achievement

Goal pursuit

Goal pursuit is where long and short term goals come together. To achieve your long-term goals you need to accomplish the short-term, small goals. These tend to be clearer. The long-term goals or outcomes are usually fuzzy but provide the motivation to keep going. Goal pursuit has three components:

> A **beginning** - starting to move towards the goal. How goals are framed at this stage is important

> A **middle** - understanding the best route to achieve goals and how goals interact with each other

> An **end** - maintaining your motivation until you achieve an embedded outcome.

Understanding where you are in pursuit of achieving the goal will help to keep you on track. Elliot Berkman calls this the AME model; Aim, Move, Embed.

What to do – Using AME

Goals theory has been slow to recognize the different elements of goal setting and achievement. Goal pursuit is also a process with different strategies working better at different times. Use the different tips in this section to ensure you have strategies in each of the three parts of the goals process:

> **Aim -** See tips on Avoid/Approach, Know Yourself, Why/How goals
> **Move -** See tips on If/Then Strategies, Triggers, Meta-Cognition
> **Embed -** See tips on Know Yourself, Rewards and Behavioural Habit.

The more you engage with others to help you achieve your goals, the more likely you are to be successful.

Why and how goals

To be successful it helps to create two types of goals. The first type is about **why** you want to change. The second is about **how** you will achieve the change.

How goals activate a different part of the brain than **why** goals. **Why** goals are activated in the default system, where we think about others and ourselves.

How goals are associated with the part of the brain that thinks about tactics and strategies. People can get trapped in a habit of only thinking about one or the other type of goal.

Without goals about **why**, it is harder to keep on track with the **how** goals. Without **how** goals, it is hard to make progress on **why** goals.

What to do – Creating how and why goals

Check your goals and make sure you have both types. Look particularly for **why** goals with no **how** goals. This is the most frequent mistake made when goal-setting.

Why goals are often the outcome you will achieve. The vision you have. **How** goals are the steps and milestones to achieve the outcome. If you have not created a plan about the steps you need to take to achieve the change, it is very unlikely to happen. In situations where the whole team needs to change, involving people in creating the **how** and the **why** works best.

Also see the tip on If/then statements which is another tool to move you towards achieving your goals.

Avoid or approach goals

Research has found that people tend to have a preference for how they get motivated to achieve new goals. Some people like to move away from the old situation. This motivates them to change. Other people like to move towards the new, to have a clear vision of the future. There are distinct areas in the brain which relate to the different preference.

Knowing your preference can help you form your goals correctly and maintain motivation.

What to do – Establishing your preference

To establish your preference think about the way you describe goals or performance. Do you say things like; "I'll be in big trouble if I don't get this done" - Avoid. Or "I'd like to try that, it sounds exciting" - Approach.

When writing goals it is best to frame them in the way that motivates you the most. If your preference is for Approach:

> Create a picture of the future when you will have achieved the goal. Describe the advantages in the future; how you will feel, the advantages you will have, how good it will be.

If your preference is for Avoid:

> Articulate what you want to avoid or what problem you have. Be aware it is often difficult to articulate what you *do* want. Realise your motivation may wane when you get close to achieving your goal and the problem recedes.

Thinking about goals

Being aware of your own thinking can help you to achieve your goals and hence improve your performance.

This works in two major ways. Firstly, how you describe your goals to yourself. The words and phrases you use have a subliminal effect on your motivation; they can help or hinder you. Secondly, notice how you motivate yourself to achieve the goals, particularly how you think about any slippage or set backs on your journey towards your goal. One slip does not end the attempt to achieve the goal. You may still perform well if you also put strategies in place to manage setbacks prior to needing them.

What to do – Strategies to think about goals

How do you think about your goals?

+ **Self-talk.** Do you talk to yourself about your goals and performance? Is the dialogue motivating or do you think about how difficult and painful the goals are? Whether your preference is for towards or away from your goals you should still talk positively
+ **Know own biases.** Historically, where do you usually get stuck, fail or go off track? What can you do to anticipate and mitigate this tendency?
+ **Know what works**. What strategies have worked for you in the past? Consider if the degree to which you share goals with others makes a difference, how much you rely on others to keep you motivated, what rewards work best for you?
+ **Create a habit**. How can you ensure the outcome of the goal has become a new habit, something you do automatically?

Triggers and stickiness

One of the strategies to achieve your goals is to remember them! Research has found that it helps to link goals to things which are easily memorable. We remember things that come to mind easily, these can be said to be sticky. Research by Elliot Berkman has shown that things that are in the present are easier to remember. Things that are in the future or conceptual are harder to remember. Goals tend to be conceptual and future-oriented. Remembering goals therefore takes more effort in the pre frontal cortex.

Research is limited but shows that if there is an association for you between a trigger, a situation, event, time of day, a person or action you regularly do, this makes the goal easier to remember and prompts you. The more you can make the action you have to take to achieve the goal automatic, the more likely you are to keep on track with the goal.

What to do – Creating goal prompts

Clearly write down your goals. The more detail in which you describe the goal the clearer it becomes. Use language that is multisensory and gives you an emotional as well as a rational sense of the goal.

Next associate an action with the goal, identify when you will do the action to achieve the goal and when it is not applicable. This might be a sticky note on your computer to remind you, it might be a routine you adopt or a practice each morning or similar.

Repeat the action and goal until they become automatic. You do them without consciously thinking about them.

Commitment to the goal

When we talk about being committed to achieving a goal there is both a cognitive and a physiological component to that statement. We feel the commitment in our body. Where we feel this - usually somewhere between the neck and the navel. There may also be a picture, or dialogue associated with the commitment to the goal.

Checking these can tell you the level of real commitment to the goal i.e. whether you are aiming for something you feel you should do rather than something you really want to do.

These cognitive and physiological messages can indicate if you need to adjust your goal or change it.

What to do – Checking commitment signals

It's not unusual to set a goal but never quite get round to doing it. Checking you are actually committed to achieving your goal can save a lot of time and frustration:

+ Recall a goal that you were absolutely committed to. You knew you would do it
+ Notice where you feel that sense of commitment in your body
+ Fully describe the feeling out loud
+ Shake yourself and remove the feeling
+ Now imagine working on your current goal. Notice whether you feel the same sense of commitment in the same part of your body.

If not, revisit your goal and adjust it until you have the commitment feeling.

If/then strategies

Working towards achieving your goals works better if you have strategies to deal with times when temptation may drive you off track on goal progress.

People who have if/then implementation strategies have been found to be more likely to achieve their goals. If/then strategies describe what you will do if a situation occurs which could lead you away from your path to achieving a goal.

Research has found having the strategy prepared in advance makes it more likely that you will remember it and act on it. This is a technique that can also work for team goals. It requires putting together a plan of the potential challenges and what might trip up the team's progress.

What to do – Creating if /then strategies

Once you have clearly articulated your goal, make a plan of how you will achieve the goal, the steps and short-term goals that will take you there. Next, think about when you may be tempted to do something that moves you away from achieving your goal, such as eating cake if your goal is to lose weight.

Now create an if/then strategy. For example "if I am offered a piece of cake, then I will ask for fruit." Having the strategy worked out in advance makes it easier to recall and implement when temptation strikes.

For the team, work together to identify all the challenges and potential roadblocks and come up with a plan to overcome them should they occur.

Maintain motivation to achieve goals

One thing that keeps us on track against our goals is receiving rewards. For the brain, this means a shot of dopamine. We can increase the likelihood of this, if we design goals to indicate when we have made progress or achieved a milestone. This way the brain receives a shot of dopamine at more frequent intervals, at each milestone rather than at the achievement of the final outcome.

But be careful! Dopamine is activated in anticipation of the reward. If the reward is not then experienced, there is a drop and an error activation which creates a sense of threat in the brain.

This applies to team goals to. Be clear about how you will reward your team and when, and make sure you celebrate when your team has achieved their milestones to keep dopamine working for you and your team.

What to do – Celebrating progress toward a goal

Once you or your team start to see results as progress is made towards goals, you are much more likely to keep moving forward. Seeing results motivates. Structure goals to help maintain motivation:

+ Break the goal down into 10 steps, the tenth step being completion of the goal
+ List actions that will move you/them from step one to ten
+ Make a note of which step you/they are currently on. Some progress may already have been made (which will cause an immediate dopamine surge)
+ As each step is achieved, congratulate yourself/them. Notice how good it feels to have achieved the step
+ Check whether new developments require you/them to adjust their plan.

Using anticipation

Scientists set up a series of experiments with monkeys to explore the connection between reward and anticipation. The experiments involved a signal which prompted the monkey to undertake a task and on completion receive a reward. Initially, dopamine was produced on receipt of the reward. The interesting finding was that once the monkey became familiar with the task, dopamine was released when the signal was given rather than when they received the reward, implying that the anticipation of the reward is more motivating than the actual reward. Furthermore, if there is uncertainty about receiving the reward then dopamine levels increase significantly.

Unexpected rewards deliver the biggest shot of dopamine and hence the biggest reward.

What to do – Creating robust rewards

Consider these questions to check you have a robust reward plan in place:

+ What are the main steps and milestones associated with your team's goals?
+ How can you help your team to remember to think about the reward and anticipate receiving it?
+ Make a note of each reward at each milestone and help them to visualise themselves enjoying the reward
+ How can you introduce an element of "maybe" into the rewards that you deliver?
+ How can you deliver unexpected rewards?

Working on goals with others

The more you perceive others as similar and the closer you feel to the other people you work with, the more likely you are to be able to achieve goals. This has been called 'My progress is their progress.'

Research found brain responses in watching others were different than when watching a friend. In the friend situation there was more activation to learn from them and increased performance was later observed. People also learnt from friends' mistakes more than from general observation of others.

What to do – Achieving goals together

Take actions to form teams who know each other well and see themselves as similar:

+ Facilitate a common purpose
+ Have people form the goals themselves and the route to achieve the goals
+ Use technology that helps people connect such as social networking-type software
+ Use group pressure to remind people of the goal, and their role
+ Reward effort (growth mind-set) and achievement.

Priming success

The goals we pursue are not always created by our conscious mind. In a paper that attracted a lot of media attention, Rudd Custer and others examined research that showed that the pursuit of goals often happens out of conscious awareness. Furthermore the pursuit of goals can be impacted by the environment. People may be more warm and friendly when holding a hot cup of coffee or are tougher in a negotiation when sitting on a hard chair.

It is not only goals that can be impacted in this way. Experiments exposing people to cue words with positive associations such as warm, beach, laughter resulted in harder work and more persistence to solve a problem than a control group who were exposed to neutral words.

What to do – Using belief to achieve goals

Have people list the beliefs they have about the project or goal.

Divide the beliefs into those that are limiting, that is they are about why the goal cannot be done, or will be difficult, and those that are enabling, that is they will help the goal to happen.

Taking the limiting beliefs, ask people to find evidence that these beliefs are false. Ask you colleagues to coach each other if people get stuck.

Pick three useful, empowering beliefs that will help people to be more successful. Find evidence that these beliefs are true. Again ask your colleagues to assist each other when people are stuck. Imagine that the new positive beliefs are true. Try this out by having people walk around the room and say one of the beliefs to each other. Keep going until it feels natural to say the belief. Find ways to reinforce these beliefs back at work.

Know your self

We all play many roles in life. Some roles feel easy and familiar and others are a bit more of a stretch. Understanding who you are in each role and how you flex and change is one way of getting comfortable in your own skin. This sense of comfort is often seen by others as authenticity.

What to do – Knowing your many roles

You can come to know yourself better through the roles you play in the world. Exploring your roles can help you to fulfil your long-term goals. Make a list of your roles in life: parent, spouse, professional, sibling...

For each role ask yourself:

+ How much of me is expressed through this role?
+ What do I tend to emphasise in this role? What do I downplay?
+ Now look over the results and consider these questions:
+ In which roles are you most fully yourself?
+ Which ones bring out the best in you?
+ Which help you achieve your long terms goals? What is it about these roles that enable you to achieve long-term goals? How do you see yourself in these roles?
+ How can you take these insights and use them more?

Monitor the changes you make and reward yourself for successful achievement.

Creating new behavioural habits

Our brain developed to be very energy efficient. One of the features is that routine behaviours are run by the basal ganglia in the form of habits. These are short cuts that allow you to do things without thinking about them each time. Whilst this is efficient, it also makes it hard to change behaviours when your current habits are no longer useful. It is better to start a new habit than to stop an ingrained one.

Conventional wisdom says it takes three months to form a new habit but this is not proven and the quality of the elements in learning the new behaviour and embedding the change is more important than the time.

What to do – Building new habits

Habits have three elements:

> **The cue** - this signals you to start the habitual behaviour
>
> **The reward** - the sense you get that keeps you performing the behaviour. It is not always easy to recognise this
>
> **The routine** - the ritual you perform or steps in your habitual behaviour.

Understand what each of these elements is in your new target behaviour. In particular, be clear about the reward. It may be useful to understand the reward you got from the old behavior and replicate or replace it in the new. Keep at the new behaviour until you do it frequently without thinking about it. Test this in stressful circumstances not just easy ones.

Your future self

The economic model of behaviour suggests we make rational decisions based on our goals. So if we want to lose weight we will stop eating cake. Yet we all know this is not what actually happens.

Science is coming up with a different hypothesis, that actually we make a comparison between ourselves now and ourselves in the future; our self when we have lost the weight. Some of us think about our future self like we think about another person. This can lead us to make predictions that our future self will want different things to our current self. How well we can predict our future self; what will reward and motivate us will determine whether we stick to our goals or succumb to temptation? One of the things that will impact our ability to change is how well we know what things help us stay on course or what will trip us up.

What to do – A letter from your future self

One way to overcome this disconnect is to spend time getting to know the future you. Imagine how you will be, what will be important to you and in doing so you can also help to create the future you want. For example write a letter from your future self about a current challenge and how you managed it and say thank you for the actions you took. It is best to be optimistic. It's not about being exactly the same but that you are emotionally connected to the future you.

Research suggests in reality we change very little so making the future real is probably easier than we think.

THE SCIENCE OF INFLUENCE

Getting buy-in to your ideas

The science of Influence

Many scientific experiments have pointed to a number of tactics that work to improve your chances of influencing others; something which is constantly needed by the leader in times of change. Scientist Robert Cialdini has summarised these as the six tactics of persuasion. They are:

> Reciprocity
> Commitment and consistency
> Social proof
> Liking and likeness
> Authority
> Scarcity

Employing one or more of these tactics can help you influence.

What to do – Influence tips

In the following tips, we describe each tactic and how it may be deployed. All you need to do is decide which tactic would be most appropriate for the issue and plan how to incorporate it.

Just one thing to remember! Influence works when we are doing it for the right motives, whilst con artists use many of these tactics, leaders use them for good, not selfish motives.

Reciprocity

Evolutionary scientists believe this rule developed to aid survival. If you do something for one of the group they in turn owe you and when, for example, the next animal is killed for food you get some of the meat. Alongside the give and take rule is the cultural distaste for those who break it. This is where its real power lies. As humans we need to be part of the group. If we take and do not give, we risk being ostracized or even ejected from the group.

What to do – Using reciprocity

If you want to influence a colleague think about what you have done for them and how you can remind them of the debt. If they don't owe you, consider what you can help them with before your request. Alternatively, what are you willing to give them in return for their support? Or what concession can you make that prompts them to make a return concession?

Reciprocity works best when it is payment in kind rather than cash.

Remember, when someone does something for you, ensure you keep the credit 'in the bank' so rather than say "No problem, that's ok," say "Thanks, I know you would do the same for me." You have just added a reciprocity credit to your account.

Commitment and consistency

These rules work together. We like to be consistent about what we agree, say and do. This is valued in business. Our brain also likes to be able to predict our behaviour and that of others. This drives consistency in groups and society as a whole.

Commitments are most effective when they are made willingly, are active, take some effort, are public and when the person feels they had choice. That is they were internally motivated to make the commitment and not coerced.

What to do – Using these rules

The key is to gain a commitment. Once committed people like to be consistent and are more likely to do what they say, to act in a way that is consistent with the agreement. To help a person commit:

+ Help them see the benefits for them personally
+ Link the idea to something they know already
+ Use questions to help them take a new perspective, one that matches your needs.

But take care; one commitment can lead to lots of new reasons to support the commitment. Make sure you have thought about the connecting actions that may derive from the initial commitment.

Social Proof

One means of influencing is to tap into the desire to know that others also believe or have acted in the same way. As humans, two factors are at play here:

+ The desire to conform to the norms of our current in-group
+ Or to join a group by acting like them.

Social proof works best when people are uncertain or the situation is ambiguous and there is not clear data. The second condition is when there is similarity between the examples of social proof and the person you want to influence.

At a brain level, both conditions reduce the level of threat in the brain created by uncertainty.

What to do – Using social proof

When using social proof to influence consider:

+ The other groups or stakeholders who have already agreed to your proposal. How will your target stakeholder view their agreement?
+ What data supports your proposal? What is the best way to bring this information to the attention of your target? Should this be direct information you include in your proposal or more indirect?

Remember social proof may work against you if there is not trust or respect between the person you are trying to influence and the data or group you are citing.

Liking and likeness

People prefer to agree with a proposition if they like you. This seems intuitively obvious and forms a part of many business relationships. The research also shows that the more attractive people are the more persuasive they are and the more similar they are the more influential. In-group/ out-group categorization is at play here. We assume people who are similar to us in one way are similar in many ways. This is known as the False Consensus Effect (see Brain Basics).

Another way in which liking works in aiding persuasion is when people are familiar with the person or the proposal. This reduces uncertainty in the brain and places you in the target's in-group, at least on some criteria. This works even better if the contact takes place in positive circumstances so the familiarity is also associated with other pleasant anchors.

What to do – Getting to know stakeholders

Think about these questions and plan them into your approach:

+ How can you get to know the person you want to influence?
+ Do you understand what is important to them and does your proposal demonstrate your understanding and address what is important to them?
+ How can you make the proposal feel familiar or increase familiarity prior to the decision?
+ Have you identified and used factors in your proposal that they already like. For example an existing policy or your stakeholder's values?
+ How similar are you, what shared interests do you have?

Are there ways that you can work together on the proposal or the implementation for the greater success of you both?

Authority

There are many examples in society of people acting, often against their own interests at the request of an authority figure. The brain is influenced by symbols of status such as titles and clothes. People also crave and are rewarded by enhanced reputation. Being associated with an authority is one way to enhance your reputation in influence situations. In addition, people are socialised to respect and follow authority which in some circumstances means people automatically follow.

People tend to underestimate the impact of authority and especially authority symbols on them and their tendency to be influenced.

What to do – Using the authority rule

There are many ways to use authority to influence in business:

+   What is your own standing? What are you an authority on and how will this help you influence?
+   Are there authorities within the company you can co-opt to your cause? How can you use these authorities in your influence plan?
+   How to use external authorities? If you can't have them personally present how else can you introduce them? Via video, examples on the internet, articles etc
+   What symbols are you using in your influence plan? Have you the right authority symbols? In many companies the internal branding and channel of communication carry an authority. Have you used the right ones?

Scarcity

People assign more value to an object or opportunity that is scarce or where there is limited availability. We see this all the time: high potential programmes open to just a few, shares for retention again to a few, and limited time to sign up for leadership programmes. This works because we are socialised to think what is scarce is valuable. Secondly our brains like options, to have choice, and as things become scarcer we have less choice and therefore want the opportunity or object more. This scarcity principle also applies to information. By limiting access to information, people want it more. Of course, the internet and Twitter have made this more of a challenge.

What to do – Creating a sense of scarcity

Consider these questions in your influence plan:

+   Is there a natural scarcity of objects or information in your proposal? How can you use this in your influence plan?
+   What other things are scarce, like your time, your information, your expertise. How can you use these?

Consider how you can introduce a sense of scarcity alongside other influence tactics suggested in these tips.

Spread the word

Research by Matt Lieberman indicates that if we want a message to be spread by others you need to engage the areas of the brain that work out how others feel and what is important to them. This is called the mentalizing network or default network. To activate this, people need to be able to put themselves in others' shoes and think about how others would view the new information, not just know and understand the information.

What to do – Getting into others shoes

Rather than just focusing on the content of your message think about how others will receive it. If you were in their shoes:

+ What would resonate?
+ What would engage?
+ How excited will they feel?
+ What would the key points be to make them interested?

Plan how you can pass on information in a way that engages their thinking about others not just their memory of the details.

MANAGING YOUR OWN PERFORMANCE

Everything from exercise to sleep and mindfulness

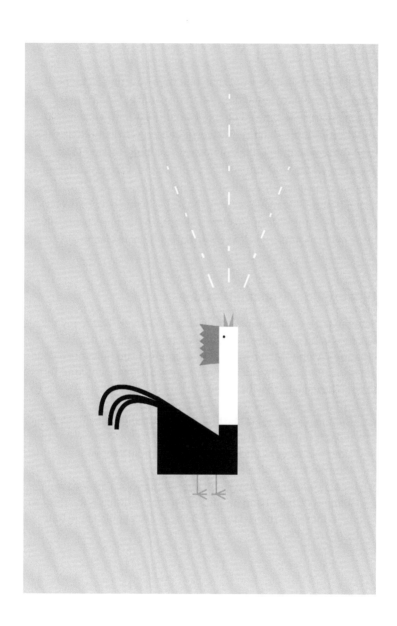

Multi-tasking myth

We all think we can do more than one thing at a time. Our busy jobs often seem to demand it. Yet in research at Stanford University, results showed people who thought of themselves as 'multi-taskers' did significantly worse at trying to do multiple things than those who didn't think that way. The multi-taskers took longer to switch from one task to another and were less efficient at juggling problems. Research at the University of London has also found that multi-tasking reduces the IQ by as much as 10 points (about the same as losing a night's sleep), and reduces productivity by as much as 40% as well as contributing to increased errors.

What to do – Stop multitasking

Set yourself a goal of not multi-tasking for a week. For many this will be a habit and quite difficult to do (see the tip on habit creation). Monitor the results of how you feel and how much you get done. Particularly, notice the progress on important long-term tasks. These ideas may help you:

+ Get engaged; people start multi-tasking when they think their input is not necessary
+ Limit exposure to information that might attract your attention. Turn off electronic alerts
+ For a 24-hour period turn off everything with a screen: your computer, tablet and phone. Keep them out of sight. This can be unnerving, so prepare in advance. Let people know that you are off-line.

Say no to distractions

Our brain is constantly alert to new, unexpected information. This scanning developed as a survival mechanism in the older brain regions which developed to alert us when something unexpected might signal danger. In the modern world, this is often misused; for example the ping of an email is tapping into this region of the brain and distracting other parts of the brain from more complex tasks.

Distractions exhaust the pre frontal cortex's limited resources. Whilst we do have a breaking system to resist the distractions, this takes massive energy and quickly gets exhausted.

What to do – Turn off distractions

This tip is deceptively simple and yet very difficult for most people to do.

The distractions are a habit, removing them creates uncertainty:

+ Remove external distractions: turn off email, and all devices
+ Plan a period of time when you will work in this way. Gradually increase the time period over which you do this
+ Reduce internal distractions by clearing your mind before starting on difficult tasks. Pick an aspect of the task and focus on that
+ Plan for distractions that may occur and inhibit them early before they gain momentum. Set if/then strategies to overcome the interruptions.

Name that emotion

One of the strategies often used to control our emotions is suppression, or as it is called in the UK, the "stiff upper lip" strategy. Whilst this can be partially successful on the outside, there is an internal cost. Suppression tends to increase the strength of the emotion internally and depletes our mental resources. We are also likely to have worse memories of the emotion. This creates consequences over time especially to our health and cognitive functioning. Rather than suppressing the emotion, scientists have shown that labelling the emotion can be a much more beneficial strategy. fMRI scans show that when participants label the emotion using words, less activity occurs in the amygdala - the area of the brain involved in emotion.

What to do – Name the emotion

Use these steps when you anticipate experiencing a difficult emotion or as you are feeling it:

+ Give the emotion a name. Something that you recognise. It does not have to be a name everyone would use; you can create your own
+ If you find it difficult to name the emotion just make a name up
+ Say the name to yourself, write it down, and draw a picture. Anything that gets it out
+ Step back and notice how you feel.

This is deceptively simple but neuroscience research shows it works!

Who gets in your way?

Science is showing that we think of ourselves in different ways depending on the context. We have the person who wants to change and the person who wants to stay the same; the overtired irritable person who stays at work late and the fun-loving person who wants to see friends and relax. When we set an intension to change, which 'person' wins out will depend on how well we can keep on track with our desires rather than our immediate temptations.

What to do - Manage gremlins

One way to know ourselves is to think about our gremlins. Gremlins are those parts of our inner self that stop us being the best we can be. Most of these parts started with a positive intention; one that wants to protect us. Getting to know your gremlins lets you benefit from the positive whilst limiting the negative impact:

+ Write down the gremlins you have
+ Give each one a name
+ What are they trying to protect you from?
+ What would be a more helpful way to get this protection without compromising your goals?

Sometimes just acknowledging the gremlin reduces its negative impact.

Learning from competitors

Research at Bristol University in the UK has found that rather than learning from others successes, we learn from their failures. In an experiment, when players saw their competitors gain there was little brain activity but when they saw them lose, parts of the brain associated with inhibition were strongly activated. This suggests that learning from the competition is focused on avoiding their mistakes.

In the study researchers found that when the 'competitor' (actually a computer) made their move, the area associated with mirror neurons, which respond to the actions of others, was active, as if the player was making the same choices. When the competitor failed the areas associated with inhibition were active suggesting stopping, responding in kind.

What to do – Share mistakes

Who do you learn from? We have all been encouraged to look for role models but maybe we should be looking for negative models; those we can learn from to avoid failure. Think about the boss you know you definitely don't want to emulate. Often I have heard people say they have learnt more from a poor boss than a good one and this may now be backed up by the research.

The other way of thinking about this research is how do you help your team learn from your mistakes and the mistakes of other team members, by being open about them rather than trying to cover them up? Encourage the sharing of mistakes; not just what they were but how they happened so that the team can activate their mirror circuits and learn from it.

Willpower

Willpower is usually associated with stopping yourself doing something. Like eating chocolate or taking another glass of wine. But willpower can also be about saying yes to long-term goals or desire. Being healthy or your ideal weight. So willpower may be about what you will do or what you won't do or what you want. Consider each of these before forming your goals and strategies for change.

What to do – Understand the nature of the challenge

The following questions will help you identify the type of challenge you want to take on:

"I will" challenge. What is something that you would like to do more of or stop putting off? These types of challenges usually improve your life.

"I won't" challenge. What is the most embedded habit in your life? What would you like to stop or do less of because it undermines your quality of life? For example, your health, happiness or success.

"I want" challenge. This is about your long-term goals. What is the long term goal that creates a sense of excitement and energy? What immediate 'want' is most likely to distract you or move you away from this goal?

True grit

For decades science and industry have been trying to develop tests and definitions of what traits will ensure success in life and business. IQ is probably the most well-known and in some fields becoming the most controversial. One problem with this research is that most personality traits are vaguely defined. Psychologist Angela Duckworth decided to narrow down the criteria and focus on grit. Grit is about picking a goal and sticking with it. Her study finds that those who persist are more likely to succeed. Duckworth is also beginning to look at whether grit can be trained. You can take her the survey at www.gritstudy.com and learn how much grit you have.

What to do – Training persistence

Create a culture of improving continuously and sticking with goals until they are achieved or obsolete. Successful people continually seek to improve their performance. One simple method for doing this is the 30-second debrief.

On completion of a task, meeting or interaction ask yourself (or ask one of your team) these questions:

+ What went well? How can you do more of this next time?
+ What could have gone better? What is the learning?
+ How will you use the learning and what went well to improve next time?

Managing energy

According to David Rock, the consultant who specialises in using neuroscience, we can significantly improve the quality of our thinking (and therefore our value to the business) by understanding the biological limitations of our brain and then tailoring our work style to accommodating those limitations.

Our conscious thinking activities are intensive users of the executive brain or the pre frontal cortex. This area has limited capacity because it uses so much energy; like a battery it loses power as we use it. Each time we consciously think about something, we deplete the battery and the weaker the battery, the lower the quality of our thinking. If we want to maximise our performance, we must manage our mental energy use.

What to do – Preserving brain energy

Here are some ways to manage your brain more efficiently:

+ Start the day with planning and prioritising a "to do" list. Work on the most important and challenging tasks first since they need the most energy and focus and then your mind will be fresh
+ Turn off distractions before they take over - close down email, switch phone on to silent, turn off alerts and ask not to be disturbed unless it's an emergency
+ Avoid scheduling meetings at a time of day that you know you will be more tired
+ Take a break for 5 minutes, take a stretch, walk round the office or grab a glass of water.

Sleep

Researcher Jessica Payne, at the University of Notre Dame, studies the impact of sleep and stress on memory and cognitive functioning. Her studies include how disturbance in sleep influences memory consolidation and how this in turn influences cognitive functioning. Payne has found that lack of sleep impacts performance on cognitive tasks to an alarming degree. So, for example, the quality of decision-making will be impacted negatively. Scientists believe that our brains consolidate learning and memories during sleep. Studies have shown that people who don't sleep enough, have more trouble learning new information, whilst sleeping well helps the brain effectively put new information into long-term memory. Jessica maintains that a lack of sleep can have the same impact as drinking alcohol on our cognitive abilities at work.

What to do – Better sleep

To maximise your performance and wellbeing:

+ Make sleep a priority even if you are tempted to stay up late. Sleep has restorative qualities and you will work more efficiently the next day
+ Create a ritual or habit that optimises your ability to sleep. If you've been working, frazzled and rushing throughout your day, have some wind-down time, disengage and calm your mind for at least an hour before you get into bed
+ If you have trouble getting to sleep, try slow, deep breathing or relaxation techniques, such as stretching or meditation, to calm your mind.

Flow

According to Jessica Payne, at the University of Notre Dame, mild stress or Flow is one of the key ingredients of optimum learning and brain functioning, i.e. performance. Most of the work on Flow has been carried out by Csikszentmihalyi who has found that once people know how to get into Flow they find it easier to repeatedly achieve the state.

Flow is achieved when there is a balance between the level of challenge in a task and your perceived abilities to carry it out. If either is too low you coast, too high you go into panic.

These three factors (mild stress, sleep, and mood) are linked and will impact each other. So, a positive in one will tend to help achieve a positive state in the others. If you are in a good mood, you are likely to sleep better.

What to do – Creating Flow

Reduce stress but only to the point of Flow; try taking a quick walk to activate another area of the brain or write ideas down to get them "out of your head" - if there's less information, there's less activity. If you are feeling overwhelmed, divide the task into smaller chunks which are more manageable.

When you need to do the opposite and bring your adrenaline level up to the point of Flow, visualise a mild fear - fear brings on an immediate alertness. Or challenge yourself to carry out the task in a new way, using new skills. In addition:

> Have a good night's sleep

> Seek out people and things that make you happy.

Finding your sweet spot

The sweet spot is also known as the Yerkes Dobson law, or 'the inverted U'. These two scientists found that if stress is too low we suffer from apathy. If stress is too high we suffer from anxiety. Both of these states impact performance negatively. As we become more stressed, cortisol (stress hormone) floods the amygdala, the emotion centre of the brain, as well as the hippocampus, associated with memory. This explains why we often suffer from a mental block or become emotional when we are overly stressed. If we are apathetic there is insufficient dopamine (reward hormone) to generate reward and propel us to act.

The sweet spot is where we are in Flow, able to focus and motivated to achieve our goals.

What to do – Getting the right level of arousal

Firstly work out where you are on the inverted U. Is arousal too high, undermining your concentration and focus? Or is arousal too low making you feel lethargic? If under aroused:

+ Add challenge to the task
+ Do the task in a new way or using new skills
+ Reduce the time available
+ Challenge yourself to achieve a higher performance level than maybe you need or usually carry out.

If arousal is too high:

+ Break the task into smaller chunks
+ Seek input from others who are skilled
+ Increase your skill level
+ Extend the time available

How healthy is your mind?

David Rock and Dan Siegel created 'The Healthy Mind Platter', a guide consisting of seven essential mental activities necessary for optimum brain health in daily life. These seven daily activities make up the full set of mental nutrients that your brain needs to function at its best. By engaging every day in each of these servings, you promote integration in your life and enable your brain to coordinate and balance its activities, thereby strengthening your brain's internal connections and your connections with other people.

The key to using these techniques is to aim for a healthy dose of each activity each day. Like a balanced diet, there are many combinations that can work well together - experiment to discover yours.

What to do – Using the healthy mind platter

Keep a journal of the time you spend on each and adjust your activity:

Focus Time: Focus on tasks and challenges in a goal-orientated way
Play Time: Be spontaneous or creative, playfully enjoy a novel experience which makes new connections in the brain
Connecting Time: Connect with other people or the natural world activating and reinforcing the brain's relational circuitry
Physical Time: Move your body, aerobically, strengthening the brain
Time In: Quietly reflect - focusing on sensations, images, feelings and thoughts, helping to better integrate the brain
Down Time: Non-focused, without any specific goal, let your mind wander and relax
Sleep Time: Give the brain the rest it needs, we consolidate learning and recover from the experiences of the day.

Exercise

The Centre for Creative Leadership researched the link between fitness and executive performance on a number of leadership instruments. The research found there was a strong correlation between regular exercise and performance. Exercising in the morning before going to work:

+ Spikes brain activity
+ Prepares you for mental stress for the rest of the day
+ Produces increased retention of new information
+ Produces more tolerance of complex or challenging situations
+ Is linked to greater creativity and clearer thinking.

People who exercise report; thinking more clearly, feeling more positive and reflecting, as well as weight and fitness results.

What to do - Labelling exercise

One of the issues which gets in the way of creating a regular exercise programme is the way in which many people label and think about exercise. Notice how you think about exercise. Is it:

+ Something you should do rather than something you want to?
+ A chore rather than a pleasure?
+ Hard rather than easy?
+ Painful rather than beneficial?
+ Taking time away from pleasurable things rather than a pleasure in itself?
+ Associated with negative self-talk rather than encouraging self-talk?

How can you change the way you think about and label exercise?

Mindfulness

Mindfulness or to 'be mindful' means to be present in the moment, undistracted and accepting. Our ability to pause before we react, says Dan Siegel. It gives us the space of mind in which we can consider options and then choose. As a leader, being skilled in mindfulness helps you notice connections, focus on important data and to be more aware of others' concerns and emotions as well as being able to monitor your own moods and reactions to events. When you listen to a hunch to plan your day better, you're being mindful. When you reflect on your mood and whether it will help you achieve the results, you are being mindful. Research has shown that brain activity begins to change within just a few days of practicing mindfulness, decreasing stress, and improving your mood and ability to step back from emotional events and take a more considered perspective.

What to do – Everyday mindfulness

To understand the difference between carrying out a task mindfully rather than mindlessly set the intention to clean your teeth mindfully:

+ Notice every action, feeling and sound
+ Notice the difference between your normal pattern
+ Monitor how you will drift and get caught up thinking about something else. Bring your attention back to your teeth cleaning.

Now practice this with other routine tasks. Start with short time periods and build up time. You can practice:

In the gym, walking to the train, on the train, eating, drinking your coffee and virtually any other activity.

To try a more focused practice download the app 'Get some head space' which is an easy-to-learn meditation. Then over time notice the impact on your reactions and stress levels.

Further reading

If you want to delve a bit deeper here are a list of books that have been used to compile the science:

Dan Ariely (2009). Predictably Irrational: The Hidden Forces that Shape Our Decisions. *HarperCollins.*

Dan Ariely (2012). The (Honest) Truth About Dishonesty: How We Lie to Everyone - Especially Ourselves. *Harper.*

Roy Baumeister and John Tierney (2011). Willpower: Rediscovering the greatest human strength. *Penguin.*

Bechara A, Damasio H, Damasio AR (March 2000). Emotion, decision making and the orbitofrontal cortex. *Cerebral Cortex 10(3).*

Robert Burton (2008). On Being Certain: Believing You Are Right Even When You're Not. *St Martin's Press.*

Mihaly Csikszentmihalyi (2008*). Flow: The Psychology of Optimal Experience. Harper Perennial.*

Guy Claxton 1999 Hare Brain, Tortoise Mind: How Intelligence Increases When You Think Less. *Harper Perennial*

Antonio Damasio (1994). Descartes' Error: Emotion, Reason, and the Human Brain. *Putnam Adult.*

Carol Dweck (2006). Mindset: The New Psychology of Success. *Random House.*

Charles Duhigg (2012). The Power of Habit. *Random House.*

Barbara Frederickson (2009). Positivity: Groundbreaking Research Reveals How to Embrace the Hidden Strength of Positive Emotions, Overcome Negativity, and Thrive. *Crown Archetype.*

Adam Grant (2013). Give and Take: A Revolutionary Approach to Success. *Weidenfeld & Nicolson.*

Jon Kabat-Zinn (1994). Wherever You Go, There You Are: Mindfulness Meditation in Everyday Life. *Hyperion.*

Daniel Kahneman (2011). Thinking Fast and Slow. *Farrar, Straus and Giroux.*

Matthew Lieberman (2013). Social: Why our brains are wired to connect. *Oxford University Press.*

John Medina (2008). Brain Rules: 12 principles for surviving and Thriving at Work, Home, and School. *Pear Press.*

Nick Morgan Power cues: The subtle science of leading groups, persuading others, and maximizing your personal impact. *Harvard Business Review Press*

Daniel Pink (2009). *Drive: the surprising truth about what motivates us. Riverhead.*

John J. Ratey 2002 A User's Guide to the Brain: Perception, Attention, and the Four Theaters of the Brain. *Vintage*

David Rock (2009). Your Brain at Work: Strategies for Overcoming Distraction, Regaining Focus, and Working Smarter All Day Long. *HarperBusiness.*

Simon Sinek (2009). Start with Why: How Great Leaders Inspire Everyone to Take Action. *Portfolio*

Other resources

You can find a number of videos and articles related to the content of this book at www.headheartbrain.com

Our books

Brain-savvy business: 8 principles from neuroscience and how to apply them

Brain-Savvy HR: A neuroscience evidence base is available on Amazon in paper or Kindle format

Index